Biography

David Cason, born in 1957, was raised in South Africa of British parents. The family emigrated when he was five years old and he spent his childhood initially in Cape Town, then Johannesburg, completing his schooling and entered the University of Witwatersrand in 1977. He studied biological sciences finally gaining a Ph.D. ten years later.

He moved back to the UK in 1988 where he continued his studies, completing post-doctoral research at Oxford, after which he decided he was not cut off for academic life and found a job with Proctor & Gamble based in Newcastle-upon-Tyne.

His first book, *One Mans Journey*, followed. A novel set in the height of the Apartheid era in South Africa during the 1970s dealing with the tensions of love across the colour bar.

Meet the Germans, his second book, evolved out of the many insights into the minutiae of daily life in Germany, while living in Frankfurt, where life is viewed from quite differently from the Anglo-Saxons on their island.

Meet the English, his third book, is based on a move back to the land of his birth. Observations on the habits and quirks of his fellow countrymen seen through new eyes, a stranger's perspective in his own country, have evolved into this publication.

Equity Investment Strategies his fourth book, is based on a compilation of insights culled from the writings of master equity investors sharing their secrets with the rank and file who wish to boost their portfolios

Equity Investment Strategies

Equity Investment Strategies

David Cason

DTC Publishers
2016

Equity Investment Strategies

First Printing: 2016

ISBN 978-1-226-77685-5

DTC PUBLISHERS
cason724@gmail.com

Ordering Information:
Special discounts are available on quantity purchases by corporations, associations, educators, and others. For details, contact the publisher at the above email address.

U.S. trade bookstores and wholesalers:
Please email cason724@gmail.com

To Britta and Spooky

Who provide love and support and keep me sane

Foreword

Equity investing has been a consuming passion of mine for several decades; I find the workings of the markets, the way stocks rise and fall in price and the underlying factors that drive their movements a fascinating mystery. Curiously, everything that appears counter-intuitive to the way the human mind works, is encapsulated in the daily movements of stocks in the markets. This is probably the reason so many hobby investors think they can beat the index, but end up delivering losses to their portfolios.

Part of my quest to better understand the drivers behind stock movements has been to extensively read the thoughts of others. Expert investors who are much smarter than myself, more successful in accumulating wealth in the markets. I have tried to gleam some nuggets of wisdom, key insights on how the markets operate.

The content of this book is therefore not my own. I have simply read a lot and captured the insights of others and compiled them into this book.

In the world of investment advice, there are many spin doctors and snake oil salesmen. I have tried to sift the good from the mediocre and downright bad. The thoughts here are those that touched me when reading them, they stood out and made sense. I felt they were worth keeping:-. simple but precise lists that captured the core ideas of the investment strategist in question.

I have found these insights really helpful; they moved me forward in my equity investing. I hope they help you too.

Equity Investment Strategies

Contents

Chapter 1: Equity Investment Strategies

STANLEY KROLLS SYSTEM:

1. Wait until a major trend is established, and then do your buying or selling against periods of correction within the trend. Liquidate your position when the position finally ends.

2. Don't pyramid your position i.e. increase the size of your position with bigger investments after the initial one is made. Rather add to the position in decreasingly smaller amounts so if the trend turns early you don't lose everything, but only the last few small bets.

3. Never argue with the market. If the trend turns against you, just sell out and walk away and reconsider.

4. Only trade the major movements

5. Only trade when the whole pattern, - i.e. upward trend - appears obvious.

6. Don't trade when there is a lot of volatility in the market.

7. Fix a strategy and stick with it. Never deviate from it. Whims and emotions are expensive.

8. It's hard to establish good positions and almost impossible to do it quickly.

FISCHER'S INVESTMENT PHILOSOPHY

1. An investor who attempts the impossible abandons his only hope of doing well.

2. You can make a lot of money by investing in an outstanding enterprise and holding it for years and years as it becomes bigger and better

3. If the job has been correctly done when the common stock was purchased, then the time to sell is - almost never. Only sell if you made a mistake in the original appraisal, and the company ceases to qualify under the original criteria used to select it

4. The silliest of all is selling out just because the share has gone up alot. The truly great company will grow on and on and its share price likewise.

COMMON TRAITS OF MASTER INVESTORS

1. They are realistic.

2. They are intelligent to the point of genius.

3. They are utterly dedicated to their craft

4. They are disciplined and patient

5. They are loners

FURTHER OBSERVATIONS

1. Within the craft one must not waste one's skill and time on un-productive inquiries or anything else that cuts the time available to do what works.

2. Stick to one's basic method

3. One should abandon unobtainable objectives such as trying to make money in short term trading

4. Patience comes from knowledge and discipline and is the hall-mark of the professional. If you know you are right, it is not hard to wait. If you don't know and are not disciplined, you risk getting shaken out at precisely the wrong time.

5. The loner's truth is within himself. Great leader's artists and thinkers have to be loners. It's often very hard to serenely do the opposite of the herd, even though it the strongest of human in-stincts.

JOHN TRAIN'S 10 POINT INVESTMENT GUIDE

1. Only buy a stock as a share in a good business that you know a lot about.

2. Buy when stocks have few friends, particularly the stock in question.

3. Be patient, don't be rattled by fluctuations.

4. Invest, don't guess.

5. High yields are often a trap.

6. Only buy what's cheap right now, or almost sure to grow so fast that it very soon will be cheap at today's price.

7. If stocks in general don't seem cheap, stand aside.

8. Keep an eye on what the masters are doing.

9. Buy investment management, if you find company analysis too difficult.

10. Decide on an appropriate investment strategy and concentrate on it.

THE WORDS OF WARREN BUFFETT

1. Buy good businesses at fair prices rather than fair businesses at good prices.

2. Price is what you pay, value is what you get

3. Risk comes from not knowing what you're doing

4. You should invest in a business that even a fool can run, because someday a fool will

5. Its only when the tide goes out that you learn who's been swimming naked

6. I would no more take an investment bankers opinion on whether to do a deal than I would ask a barber if I needed a haircut

7. If the business does well, the stock eventually follows

8. The market, like the Lord, helps those who help themselves. But, unlike the Lord, the market does not forgive those who know not what they do.

9. In a bull market, one must avoid the error of the preening duck, that quacks boastfully after a torrential rainstorm, thinking that its paddling skills have caused it to rise in the world

10. The market is there only as a reference point to see if anyone is offering to do anything foolish.

11. The value of stock forecasters is to make fortune-tellers look good.

12. I never attempt to make money on the stock market. I buy on the assumption that they could close the market the next day and not open it for five years.

13. If you feel you have to invest every day, you're going to make a lot of mistakes.

14. When management with a reputation for brilliance tackles a business with a reputation for bad economics, it is the reputation of the business that remains intact.

15. I would rather be certain of a good result than hopeful of a great one.

SIX QUALITIES NEEDED FOR INVESTIMENT SUCCESS – WARREN BUFFETT

1. You must be animated by controlled greed and fascinated by the investment process. He believes that too much greed will control you, but that too little will fail to motivate you.

2. You must have patience. His time frame is much longer than the average investor. He believes that you should buy into a company because you want to own it permanently, not because you think its stock will go up in price. His belief is that if you are right about the company, and buy it at a sensible price, you will eventually see your stocks appreciate.

3. Think independently. He believes that if you don't know enough to make your own decisions, you should not make any decisions at all. He quotes Benjamin Graham "The fact that other people disagree with you makes you neither right nor wrong. You will be right if your facts and reasoning are correct"

4. You must have the security and self confidence that comes from knowledge, without being rash or headstrong. He is telling us that if we do not have confidence in our decisions because they have been poorly thought out, we are likely to be spooked as soon as the price goes against us.

5. Accept it when you don't know something.

6. Be flexible as to the types of businesses you buy, but never pay more than they are worth.

JOHN TEMPLETONS THOUGHTS ON INVESTMENT

1. Buy stocks that others have thrown away.

2. Hold these stocks for 4 years

3. A flexible point of view is the professionals investors greatest need, and will be increasingly needed in the future

4. Always ask yourself whether a company is in an industry that is a natural target for government intervention

5. Inflation is a great problem.

6. Once a stock has moved up and is no longer a bargain, then he finds a much better buy and out goes the first one

7. 6 factors are crucially applied to all situations:

- The price earnings ratio

- Operating profit margins

- Liquidating value

- Consistent growth must be shown

- The cardinal rule is flexibility

- Don't trust rules and formula.

WILLIAM NEIL on COMMON MISTAKES MOST INVESTORS MAKE

The reason the rank and file either lose money or achieve embarrassing results is because they simply make too many mistakes.

1. Most investors never get past the starting gate because they do not use good selection criteria. They do not know what to look for to find a successful stock. Therefore they buy fourth-rate "nothing-to-write-home-about" stocks that are not acting particularly well in the marketplace and are not real market leaders.

2. A good way to ensure miserable results is to buy on the way down in price; a declining stock seems to be a real bargain because it's cheaper than it was a few months earlier.

3. An even worse habit is to average down in your buying, rather than up. If you buy a stock at $40 and then buy more at $30, and average out your cost at $35, you are following up your losers and mistakes by putting good money bad. This amateur strategy can produce serious losses and weigh you down with a few big losers.

4. The public loves to buy cheap stocks selling at low prices per share. They incorrectly feel its wiser to buy more shares of stock in round lots of 100 or 1000 shares, and this makes them feel better, perhaps more important. You would be better off buying 30 or 50 shares of higher-priced, sounder companies. You must think in terms of the number of dollars you are investing, not the number of shares you can buy. By the best merchandise available, not the poorest. The appeal of a $2, $5, or $10 stock seems irresistible. But most stocks selling for $10 or lower are there because the companies have either been inferior in the past or have had something wrong with them recently. Stocks are like anything else. You can't buy the best quality at the cheapest price.

5. First-time speculators want to make a killing in the market. They want too much, too fast, without doing the necessary study and preparation or acquiring the essential methods or skills. They are looking for an easy way to make a quick buck without spending any time or effort really learning what they are doing.

6. Mainstream America delights in buying on tips, rumours, stories, and advisory service recommendations. In other words, they are willing to risk their hard earned money on what someone else says, rather than on knowing for sure what they are doing themselves. Most rumours are false, and even if a tip was correct, the stock ironically will, in many cases, go down in price.

7. Investors buy second rate stocks because of dividends or low price-earnings ratios. Dividends are not as important as earnings per share: in fact the more a company pays in dividends, the weaker the company may be because it may have to pay high interest rates to replenish internally needed funds that were paid out in the form of dividends. An investor can lose the amount of a dividend in one or two day's fluctuation in the price of the stock. A low P/E ratio, of course, is probably low because the company's past record is inferior.

8. People buy company names they are familiar with, names they know. Just because you used to work for General Motors doesn't make it necessarily a good stock to buy. Many of the best investments will be newer names you won't know very well but could and should know if you would do a little studying and research.

9. Most investors are not able to find good information and advice. Many, if they had sound advice, would not recognize or follow it. The average friend, stockbroker, or advisory service could be a source of losing advice. It is always the exceedingly small minority of your friends, brokers or advisory services that are successful enough in the market themselves to merit your consideration. Outstanding stockbrokers or advisory services are no more frequent than are outstanding doctors, lawyers or baseball players. Only one out of nine baseball players that sign professional contracts ever make it to the big leagues. And of course, the majority of ball players that graduate from college are not even good enough to sign a professional contract.

10. Over 98% of the masses are afraid to buy a stock that is beginning to go into new ground, pricewise. It just seems too high to them. Personal feelings and opinions are far less accurate than markets.

11. The majority of unskilled investors stubbornly hold onto their losses when the losses are small and reasonable. They could get out cheaply, but being emotionally involved and human, they keep waiting and hoping until their loss gets much bigger and costs them dearly.

12. In a similar vein, investors cash in small, easy-to-take profits and hold their losers. This tactic is exactly the opposite of correct investment procedure. Investors will sell a stock with a profit before they will sell one with a loss.

13. Individual investors worry too much about taxes and commissions. Your key objective should be to first make a net profit.

---

14. The multitude speculates in options too much because they think it is a way to get rich quick. When they buy options, they incorrectly concentrate entirely in shorter-term, lower-priced options that involve greater volatility and risk than in longer-term options. Many options speculators also write naked options which are nothing but taking a great risk for a potentially small reward and therefore a relatively unsound investment procedure.

15. Novice investors alike to put price limits on their buy-and-sell orders. They rarely lace market orders. This procedure is poor because the investor is quibbling for fractions of a dollar/pound rather than emphasizing the more important and larger overall movement. Limit orders eventually result in your completely missing the market and not getting out of stocks that should be sold to avoid substantial losses.

16. Some investors have trouble making decisions to buy or sell. In other words they vacillate and can't make up their minds. They are unsure because they really don't know what they are doing. They

17. Do not have a plan, a set of principles, or rules, to guide them and therefore, are uncertain of what they should be doing.

18. Most investors cannot look at stocks objectively. They are always hoping and having favourites, and they rely on their hopes and personal opinions rather than paying attention to the opinion of the market-place, which is more frequently right.

19. Investors are usually influenced by thins that are not really crucial, such as stock splits, increased dividends, news announcements, and brokerage firm or advisory recommendations.

20. Poor principles and poor methods will yield poor results. Sound principles and sound methods will, in time, create sound results.

WILLIAM NEIL ON PRIME SELLING POINTERS

1. Buying right solves half of your selling problem. If you buy exactly at the right time off a proper base structure in the first place and do not chase or pyramid a stock when it is extended in price too far past a buy point, you will be in a position to sit through most normal corrections in the price of your stock. Winning stocks seldom dip 8% below a correct pivot -point buying price.

2. Beware of the big-block selling you see on the ticker tape just after you have bought a stock during a bull market. The selling might be emotional, uniformed, temporary, or not as large, relative to past volume, as it appears. The best of stocks can have sharp sell-offs for a few days or a week. You should refer to a chart of the stock for an overall perspective to avoid getting scared or shaken out in what may just be a normal pullback.

3. If after a stock's price is extended from a proper base, its price closes for a larger increase than on any previous up days, watch out! This move usually occurs at or very close to a stocks peak.

4. The ultimate top may occur on the heaviest volume day since the beginning of the advance.

5. Sell if a stock advance gets so active that it has a rapid price run-up for 2 or 3 weeks (8-12 days). This is called climax (blow-out) top activity.

6. Sell if a stock runs up on a stock split for 1 or 2 weeks (usually +25% or +30% and, in a few rare instances, +50%). if a stock's price is extended from its base and a stock split is announced, in many instances the stock should be sold.

7. Big investors must sell when they have buyers to absorb their stock; therefore, consider selling if a stock runs up and then good news or major publicity is released.

8. New highs on decreased or poor volume means there is temporarily no demand for the stock at that level and selling may soon overcome the stock.

9. After an advance, heavy volume without further upside price progress signals distribution.

10. Tops will show arrows pointing down on a stock daily chart (closing at lows of the daily price range on several days - in other words, full retracement of a day's advance.)

11. When it's exciting and obvious to everyone that a stock is going higher, sell, because it is too late. Jack Dreyfus said "Sell when there is an overabundance of optimism. When everyone is bubbling optimism and running around trying to get everyone else to buy, they are fully invested. At this point, all they can do is talk. They can't push the market up anymore. It takes buying power to do that". Buy when you are scared to death and others are unsure. Wait until you are happy and tickled to death to sell.

12. If a stock that has been advancing rapidly is extended from its base and opens on a gap up in price, the advance is probably near its peak. A 2 point gap in a stock's price would occur if it closed at its high of $50 for the day and the next morning opened at $52 and held above $52 during the day.

13. Sell if a stock's price breaks badly for several days and does not rally.

14. Consider to sell if a stock takes off for a good advance over several weeks and then retraces all of that advance.

15. When quarterly earnings increases slow materially or earnings actually decline for 2 consecutive quarters, in most cases sell.

16. Consider selling if there is no confirming price strength by another important member of the same group.

17. Be careful of selling on bad news or rumours; they are usually of temporary influence. Rumours are sometimes started to catch the little fish off balance.

18. Try to avoid selling on shakeouts (below major price-support areas)

19. If you didn't sell early while the stock was still advancing, sell on the way down from the peak. After the first break, some stocks may once pull back up in price.

20. After a stock declines 8% or so from its peak, in some cases examination of the previous run-up, the top, and the decline may help determine if the advance may be over or if a normal 8% to 12% correction is in progress. You may occasionally want to sell if a decline from peak exceeds 12% to 15%.

21. If a stock already has made an extended advance and suddenly makes its greatest one-day price drop since the beginning of the move, consider selling, but only if confirmed by other signals.

22. When you see initial heavy selling near the top, the next recovery will either follow through weaker in volume, show poor price recovery, or last a shorter number of days. Sell on the second or third day of a poor rally; it will be the last good chance to sell before trend lines and support areas are broken.

23. Sell if a stock closes the end of the week below a major long-term upturned line or breaks a key price-support area on overwhelming volume.

24. The number of down days in price versus up days in price will change after a stock starts down.

25. Wait for a second confirmation of major changes in the general market, and don't buy back stocks you sold just because they can be bought cheaper.

26. Learn from your past selling mistakes. Do your own post-analysis by plotting on charts your past buy-and-sell points.

27. Sell quickly before it becomes completely clear that a stock should be sold. Selling after a stock has broken an obvious support level could be a poor decision because the stock could pull back after touching off stop orders and attracting short sellers.

28. In a few cases, you should sell if a stock hits its upper channel line. (Channel lines are drawn to connect the lows and connect the highs on a stock's price chart). Stocks surging above their upper channel lines should normally be sold.

29. Sell when your stock makes a new high in price if it's off a third or fourth stage base. The third chance is seldom a charm in the market. It has become too obvious and almost everyone sees it.

30. Sell on new price highs off a wide-and-loose, erratic chart price formation.

31. Sell on highs if a stock has a weak base with much of the price work in the lower half of the base or below its 200 day moving average price line.

32. In some cases, sell if a stock breaks down on the largest weekly volume in its prior five years.

33. Some stock can be sold when they are 70% to 100% above their 200 day moving average price line.

34. After a prolonged upswing, if a stock's 200 day moving average line of its price turns into a downtrend, consider selling the stock.

35. Poor relative strength can be a reason for selling. Consider selling when a stocks relative strength on a scale from 1 to 99 drops below 70.

WHEN TO BE PATIENT AND HOLD A STOCK - WILLIAM NEIL

1. After a new purchase, draw a red defensive sell line on a daily or week graph at the precise price level where you will sell and cut your loss. In the first 1,5 to 2,5 years of a bull market, you may want to give stocks this much room on the downside and hold until the price touches the sell line before taking defensive action.

2. The defensive, loss-cutting sell line may in some instances be raised but kept below the low of the first normal correction after your initial purchase. If you raise your sell point, don't move it up too close to the current price, because any normal little weakness will shake you out of your stock. If your stock increases 15% or more after a correct purchase, move the defensive sell line up to less than 5% below the pivot purchase price.

3. I do not think you should continue to follow a stock up by raising stop-loss orders because you will be forced out near the low of an inevitable, natural correction. Once your stock is 15% above your purchase price, you can begin to concentrate on the definite price where you will sell on the way up to nail down your short term profit.

4. Your objective is to buy the best stock with the best earnings at exactly the right time and have the patience to hold it until you have been proven right or wrong. You should give stocks 13 weeks after your first purchase week before you conclude that a stock that hasn't moved is a dull, faulty selection. This, of course, applies only if the stock did not reach your defensive sell price first.

5. Any stock that rises close to 20% should never be allowed to drop back into the loss column e.g. if you buy a stock at $50 and it shoots up to $60 (+20%) and you don't take the profit when you have it, there is no intelligent reason to ever let it drop all the way back to $50 or below and create a loss. You may feel embarrassed, ridiculous, and not too bright buying at $50, watching it hit $60, and then selling at $50 to $51, but you have already made the mistake of

not taking your profit. Avoid making a second mistake and letting it develop into a loss.

6. Always pay attention to the general market. It you initiate a new purchase when the market averages are topping and beginning to reverse direction, you will likely have trouble holding the stocks bought.

7. Major advances require time to complete. Don't take profits during the first 8 weeks of a move unless the stock gets into serious trouble or is having to 2-3 week "climax" rapid run-up on a stock split. Stocks that show a 20% profit in less than 8 weeks should be held though the 8 weeks unless they are of poor quality without institutional sponsorship or strong group action. In certain cases, dramatic stocks advancing 20% or more in only 4 or 5 weeks are the most powerful stocks of all, capable of increases of 100%, 200% or more. You can try for long term moves in many of them, once your account shows a good profit and you are ahead for the year.

8. If you own a dynamic leader or a stock belonging to a leading group, you may want to hold it at least until its weekly close is below its 10-week moving average price line on increased volume. Some outstanding leaders go an amazing distance before this occurs.

9. If possible, try to hold through the stocks first short term correction once you already have a profit.

10.Holding for a long-term gain during the early stages of a new bull market, in many cases, may force you to stick to your position long enough to make a big gain. Remember, the objective is not to be right, but to make big money when you are right.

11.Investors who can be right and sit tight are uncommon. It takes time for a stock to make a big gain. The first two years of a new bull market typically provide your best and safest period for courage, patience, and profitable sitting. If you really know a company and its products well, you will have the additional confidence required to sit tight through several inevitable normal corrections. Achieving giant profits in a stock usually takes one to three years' time and patience.

THE ART OF CONTRARY THINKING - HUMPHREY NEILL

1. A group of people, or "crowd" is subject to instincts that individuals acting on their own would never be.

2. People involuntarily follow the impulses of the crowd, that is, they succumb to the herd instinct.

3. Contagion and imitation of the minority make individuals susceptible to suggestion, commands, customs, and emotional appeals.

4. When gathered as a group or crowd, people rarely reason but follow blindly and emotionally what is suggested or asserted to them.

ATTRIBUTES OF PEAK PERFORMERS - CHARLES GARFIELD

1. *A Commitment to a Mission*: This ultimate source of success was common to all respondents. In deciding their missions, peak performers have first to decide what they really care about and what they want to accomplish. The motivation for their mission is not expertise but a personal choice based on preference.

2. *Results in Real Time*: Peak performers establish realistic measurable goals and act in a deliberate manner in order to achieve them.

3. *Self-management through Self-Mastery*: Each peak performer was able to demonstrate an ability for self-observation. This involved both the ability to grab the big picture and small details. Survey participants were also able to utilize the technique of mental rehearsal in which the most desired outcome of an event and the most effective way of achieving it are first orchestrated mentally.

4. *Team Building and Team Playing:* This characteristic is but prevalent in traders and investors who act alone. But it is an important trait as well in larger organizations where it is necessary to delegate investment functions. Team builders are able to delegate to empower, stretching the abilities of others and encouraging educated risk taking.

5. *Course Correction:* this refers to the ability to initiate change and to learn from past mistakes.

6. *Change Management:* Peak performers have the ability to anticipate and deal with rapid, external changes caused by new technology or other factors and to construct alternative outcomes.

CHARACTERISTICS OF SUCCESSFUL INVESTORS – THARP

1. Money in itself is not important.

2. Investing is a game, hobby, or lover above all else.

3. Profits are a fringe benefit.

4. Losing money is accepted as part of playing the market.

5. Mental rehearsal helps in anticipating all possible outcomes.

6. A high level of self-confidence enables them to convince themselves that they have won the game before it has begun.

ATTRIBUTES OF GREAT TRADERS AND INVESTORS

1. Every successful market operator is interested in the markets and how they work, not because they promise instant or even distant wealth but because of the fascinating inner workings and the challenges they offer. Successful traders share a surprisingly large number of attitudes in regards to why they do it. Almost all claim that they do not trade for the money, but view the market as a difficult game that is changing constantly. They are by now rich and diversified enough to afford this attitude.

2. Almost all successful investors are loners. They more or less have to be, because they are constantly called on to take positions opposite to those held by the majority or by the consensus view of the market. To buy low and sell high, they must go against the market. Also they need to be creative and imaginative independent thinkers.

3. All great investors utilize a philosophy or methodology. There are many investment approaches, followed by the money masters, we find their goals - to accumulate wealth - are identical but their paths to that destination are vastly different. It does not matter which approach an investor takes as long as it works and the individual practitioner feels at home with it. Because he is comfortable with his methodology, he is able to work at it and refine it to its highest degree of efficiency. In effect, he has to be utterly dedicated to his chosen craft, for only then can he truly excel.

4. To achieve success in the markets investors must be disciplined and patient. This advice sounds so simple, yet paradoxically it is difficult to practice. Discipline means constantly gathering new facts and sticking to your rules. This is easy to achieve over the short run, but much more difficult to maintain. The only way is to work at it time and again until it becomes a habit.

5. All great market operators are realists. Once you have entered a position, there is always the temptation when things go wrong to

delude yourself that everything is still OK. This self-delusion is far less pronounced and even non-existent in successful market participants. They are quick to recognize when conditions the original reason for holding the position no longer exists. They are married to nothing and are not afraid to admit a mistake, however painful it may be at the time. They recognize that to hold on will result in even greater pain down the road. They religiously follow the rule of "cut your losses short".

6. All successful market operators seem to have the ability to think ahead and figure out what may lie ahead. This does not imply that they have a sixth sense that is unavailable to the rest of us; it is more a talent for mentally rehearsing some of the alternative scenarios. Most of us assume that the current conditions and therefore the prevailing trend in market prices will continue ad infinitum. The truly great market virtuosi on the other hand are constantly looking ahead to anticipate what could cause the prevailing trend to reverse. It is not so much that they are smarter than the rest of us, or that they are clairvoyant. Rather, they have trained themselves to question the status quo, constantly and to anticipate a possible change of course. This training is a form of mental rehearsal for the next event. All possible scenarios are examined and the unlikely ones are discarded. Then, when a change in conditions begins to take place, they are able to roll with the punches and take advantage to them. In effect, by trying to maintain a flexible outlook, the successful market operator is far less susceptible to the element of surprise.

INVESTMENT REQUIREMENTS - BOB PRECHTOR

1. A Method: An objectively defined mechanism that helps you to make an investment decision.

2. The discipline to follow the Method: Without discipline you have no method in the first place.

3. The mental fortitude to accept that losses are part of the game. Most people blame outside forces for their losses. Rarely are losses accepted as part of the game. We do not expect a baseball player to hit every ball so why should we expect to win on every trade? We should not only accept losses but also should anticipate them through sound money management.

4. The mental fortitude to accept huge gains. This is another way of saying let your profits run.

HINTS AND TIPS FROM MARTIN PRING

A.   PSYCHOLOGICAL MANAGEMENT

1. When in doubt, stay out.

2. Never trade or invest based on hope

3. Act on your own judgement entirely or else completely on the judgement of another.

4. Buy low, into weakness, sell high into strength.

5. Don't churn your portfolio.

6. After a successful and profitable campaign, take an investment vacation

7. Take a periodic mental inventory to see how you are doing

8. Constantly analyzc your mistakes

9. Don't jump the gun

10. Don't try to call every market turn

B. MONEY MANAGEMENT

1. Never enter into a position without first establishing a risk reward

2. Cut your losses, let profits run

3. Never invest more than you can reasonably afford to lose

4. Don't fight the trend

MARTIN PRING: "The process of self-critique has to be a continuous one. Do not fall into a false sense of security as profits begin to roll in. In this situation most people fall back into their old ways. You must keep the self-examination process ignited and regularly question the logic of your trades."

MARTIN PRING: "It is interesting how most people are risk adverse when it comes to taking profits and risk seeking when it comes to loses. They prefer a smaller but sure gain and are unwilling to take a wise gamble for a large gain. On the other hand, they are more willing to risk their capital for a large uncertain loss than for a certain small one."

MARTIN PRING: "When you go into an investment position, ask yourself "What is the worst that can happen?" By looking down not up, you are addressing what should be your number one objective: preserving your capital. By looking down, they are, in effect, assessing where they should cut their losses ahead of time. If they judge the potential margin of error proves to be too great, then they walk away from the investment and don't take it on. If you realize that about half of all the investment positions you are likely to take up, will probably go against you, then you must make them as inexpensive as possible and cut your losses as soon and as quickly as possible"

MARTIN PRING: "There is a well-known saying that a rising tide lifts all boats. In a market sense this is true of a bull market where most shares are likely to rise, the challenge is to find which will rise fastest"

MARTIN PRING: "Execution of an investment method requires tremendous effort. Starting out is often relatively easy because you gain strength from the initial enthusiasm gained from fresh ideas. The really hard part is the continual application of these ideas as the novelty wears off and some losses develop. The struggle to maintain newly learned disciplines is then at its most difficult."

MARTIN PRING: "The markets will continuously search out and exploit your every weakness. To overcome this challenge, you have to be constantly on guard to limit those opportunities as much as possible. Only with constant surveillance and continuous review can you accomplish this task successfully."

MARTIN PRING: "Hope is a destructive emotion which dictates your desire of the market direction, a desire often unconnected with what is actually happening in market itself. If you hope the market goes up, all indications could be it moves in the opposite direction, serious losses will be incurred"

MARTIN PRING: "There is nothing in the rule book that says you have to invest. Your impulses may encourage you to get in. Disregard them. Let your head make the decisions. It is difficult making money in the markets at the best of times so make sure that you - not the markets - decide the time has come for investing. You must have the patience to allow this to happen."

MARTIN PRING: "Keep on a predetermined and well-tested course, but also keep an open mind because underlying financial conditions can and do change."

MARTIN PRING: "It is easy to become side-stepped by events and news stories going around us. Unexpected price fluctuations stimulate our emotions and are another source of distraction. In such situations, we must make sure that we are not incorrectly drawn into believing that the main trend has reversed. A warm day in January does not mean that spring has arrived, neither does an isolated piece of good news denote that a bear market is over. We have to learn to step back and sort out the woods from the trees. If we are following a particular approach or methodology, it is important to stick with it. Otherwise we lose our basis for making sound decisions."

MARTIN PRING: "Trends occur because investors tend to move in crowds that by nature are driven by herd instincts and the desire for instant wealth. If left to their own devices, individuals isolated from the crowds would act in a far more rational way."

MARTIN PRING: "Don't get caught by the fear of missing out. The market continuously offers new opportunities, if one passed over, be patient and just wait, many more will come along."

MARTIN PRING: "Somebody who has encountered a long string of successful and profitable trades without any meaningful setbacks is *bound* to experience a feeling of well-being and a sense of invincibility. Every trader and investor goes through a cycle that alternates between success and failure. Successful traders and investors often make a deliberate effort to stay out of the market after they have experienced a profitable campaign. This "vacation" enables them to recharge their emotional batteries and subsequently return to the market in a much more objective state of mind. Investors who have had a run of success, whether from short term trading or long-term investment, have a tendency to relax and lower their guard, because they have not recently been tested by the market. When profits have been earned with very little effort, they are not appreciated as much as when you have to sweat out painful corrections and similar market contortions. Part of this phenomenon arises because a successful campaign reinforces our convictions that we are on the right path. Consequently we are less likely to question our investment or trading position even when new evidence to the contrary comes to the fore. We need to recognize that *confidence moves proportionally with prices.*"

As our confidence improves, we should take counter measures to keep our feet on the ground so that we maintain our sense of equilibrium. At the beginning of an investment campaign, this is not as much a requirement as it is as the campaign progresses, because fear and caution help rein in our tendency to make rash decisions. This means that sharp market movements that go against our position hit us by surprise. It is much better to be continually running scared and looking over our shoulder for developments that are likely to reverse the prevailing trend. Such unexpected shocks will be far less frequent because we will have learned to anticipate them. When events are anticipated, it is much easier to put them into perspective. Otherwise their true significance may be exaggerated. The idea is to maintain a sense of mental balance so that these psychological disruptions can be more easily deflected when they occur."

MARTIN PRING: "A principle lesson to learn is that good traders or investors are *always running scared*. I mean that they are always looking over their shoulder to see what new development might be affecting the markets. This does not mean that they constantly being whipped in and out of the market, nor does it mean that they must take a pessimistic view. What it does mean is that they have learned that the moment they relax and feel that they have got everything figured out they know very well that a new factor will come along to threaten their position. Their approach is not the hold-on-at-any-cost attitude engendered by pride of opinion. It is one of complete openness. That rationale is as follows "Right now I think the market is going up, but if conditions unexpectedly change and I am lucky enough to spoil it, I will change my view and liquidate" Trade for the present, but invest/plan for the future. Always have a vision of what the market direction will be in the future.

MARTIN PRING: "Most investors and speculators enter the markets believing that they can accumulate profits very quickly. This attitude means that careful consideration and planning are shoved aside and replaced by impatience and impulsiveness."

MARTIN PRING: "A major mistake by most investors is to try to call every market turn. This tactic has very little chance of success. Not only is there a tendency to lose perspective, but most of us operate in cycles, alternating between winning and losing streaks. In attempting to call every trend reversal, we invariably lose our objectivity and lose touch with the markets. It then becomes only a matter of time before we are pushed off balance psychologically. Trying to call every market turn also increases the temptation to act on impulse rather than fact. Decisions that are made infrequently are much more likely to be more thoughtful and reflective. Deliberation gives us a far greater chance of being successful than trying to call every twist and turn in the market.

Always remember: Even if a current opportunity is missed, there always will be another. The best investment decisions are made when the odds are in your favour. You increase those odds when you assess investment possibilities with a cold indifferent eye and avoid the day-to-day clutter of the marketplace."

MARTIN PRING: "You must have the will to establish a plan and follow its rules religiously. Rules won't eliminate losses, but they will help reduce the level of emotion as they increase objectivity and consistency. If you can be more objective, there will be far less room for hope, greed, and fear to crowd out your better judgement"

MARTIN PRING: "The Theory of Contrary Opinion requires us to *go against our natural instincts* - a difficult task indeed."

MARTIN PRING: "Patience, flexibility and hard work are irreplaceable allies in the quest for market success"

NINE RULES FROM BERNARD BARUCH

1. Don't speculate unless you can make it a full-time job.

2. Beware of barbers, beauticians, waiters, anyone bringing gifts of "inside" information or "tips".

3. Before you buy a stock, find everything you can about the company, its management and competitors, its earnings and possibilities for growth.

4. Don't try to buy at the bottom and sell at the top. This can't be done, - except by liars.

5. Learn how to take your losses quickly and cleanly. Don't expect to be right all the time. If you have made a mistake, cut your losses as quickly as possible.

6. Don't buy too many stocks. Better have only a few investments which can be watched.

7. Make a periodic reappraisal of all your investments to see whether changing developments have altered their prospects.

8. Always keep a good part of your capital in a cash reserve. Never invest all your funds.

9. Don't try to be a jack of all investments. Stick to the field you know best.

TEN RULES FROM ROBERT MEIER

1. Ask yourself what you really want. Many traders lose money because subconsciously their goal is entertainment, not profits. If you are serious about becoming a successful speculator, carefully examine your trading to eliminate destructive compulsiveness such as constantly calling your broker when there is no legitimate reason and putting on trades "just to be in the market"

2. Assume personal trade responsibility for all actions. A defining trait of top performing traders is their willingness to assume personal responsibility for all trading decisions. People who habitually blame

their broker, the market itself, bad order fills, or insider manipulation for losses, are never successful.

3. Keep it simple and consistent. Most speculators follow too many indicators and listen to so many different opinions that they are overwhelmed into action. Few people realize that many of the greatest traders of all time never rely on more than two or three core indicators and never listen to the opinions of others.

4. Have realistic expectations. When expectations are too high, it results in over-trading under-financed positions, and very high levels of greed and fear - making objective decision-making impossible.

5. Learn to wait. Most of the time for most speculators, it is best to be out of the markets. Generally, the part-time speculator will only encounter 6 to 10 clear-cut major opportunities a year. These are the type of trades the savvy professionals train themselves to wait for.

6. Clearly understand the Risk/Reward ratio. The consensus is that trades with a 1 to 3 or 1 to 4 Risk/Reward ratio are sufficient, but this is not true unless you are a floor trader in the pit. There are trades with Risk/Reward ratios as attractive as 1 to 10 that periodically present themselves to those willing to exercise the ongoing market monitoring discipline required. That is what professionals do.

7. Always check the big picture. Before making any trade, check it against weekly and monthly as well as daily range charts. Frequently, this extra step will identify major longer term zones of support and resistance that are not apparent on daily charts and that substantially change the perceived Risk/Reward Ratio.

8. Always under-trade. It is easy to forget just how powerful the leverage is in futures and options. It is not common to find speculators holding positions 2 to 3 times larger than is justified by their account size. By consciously under-trading, that is taking positions much smaller than you might be able to, you will gradually learn to hold

back until you find the real money-making opportunities and stay with major trends.

9. Never trade with serious personal problems. Ignoring this rule is pre-scription for disaster. The clarity of thought and emotional control required even for a part-time speculator is so great that it is impos-sible to handle along with serious personal problems. Likewise, trading should not be attempted during periods of ill health, even including a bad head cold.

10. Ignore the news media. The true goals of the national news media are to shock, agitate, entertain, and editorialize a socialist agenda - not provide useful information. Many of the finest traders avoid all contact with public news, knowing how profoundly it can undermine a trading plan. The more important trading profits are to you the less you can afford to follow the "news".

INVESTIMENT RULES - PETER WYCKOFF

1. Speculation demands cool judgement, self-reliance, courage, flexi-bility and prudence.

2. A person's planned buying plan should dovetail closely with a pre-determined selling plan.

3. When in doubt about what to do in the market, do nothing. Nothing can destroy the cool temperament of a man like un-systemic specu-lation.

4. Look after the losses and the profits will take care of themselves.

5. If you wait too long to buy, until ever uncertainty is removed and every doubt is lifted at the bottom of a market cycle, you may keep on waiting and waiting.

6. The worst losses in the market come from uninformed people buying greatly over valued stocks.

7. Whenever hope becomes a chief factor in determining a market position, sell out promptly.

8. Never buy or sell merely on the basis of background statistics. Technical market considerations and psychology must also be taken into account.

9. Don't believe everything a corporate official says about his company's stock.

10. Check all the facts carefully yourself and view them conjunctively with other known market factors.

11. Never speculate with the money you need to live. If you can't afford a possible loss, stay out of the market.

12. One way to win in the market is to avoid doing what most others are doing.

13. When opinions in Wall Street are too unanimous - BEWARE! The market is famous for doing the unexpected.

14. Try to analyze your weak points and convert them into strong ones.

15. Forget the idea that speculation depends entirely upon luck and guard against blind faith in the suggestions of other men.

16. Eliminate trust in any system you do not understand, but still believe in the basic idea of the system.

17. You should consult other market aids besides charts.

18. Never be sentimental about a stock.

19.Before investing in a stock, look into its history.

20.Always try to plan ahead, rather than considering just the last sales bobbing in front of you. The printed prices you see may have already largely discounted the news as it generally is known.

21.Be flexible at all times, but don't over-trade. Plan each campaign carefully, and never blame the tape for any error you may make.

22.You should be able to differentiate between what has been, what is now and what the future will be, in planning a trading program.

23.Before you take a position, determine exactly where the stock you are watching, or the general market, stands. A study of price, breadth, activity, time and volume will be helpful in this respect.

24.Whatever is hard to do in the market is generally the right thing: and whatever is easy usually the wrong thing to do.

25.Take a mental inventory to find out exactly where you stand.

26.Do not press yourself: ""Speculitis" is malignant!

27.When buying a stock, you should consider how far down it might carry in the event your judgement about it is wrong.

28.Buy the stocks of companies that have shown gradually increasing earnings in industries making articles that people cannot do well without.

MORE INVESTMENT RULES - FRANK J WILLIAM

1. Remember good stocks always come back - unknown stocks may disappear.

2. Small stocks are inherently more dangerous than big stocks.

3. Don't buy in a hurry. There is always time to buy good stocks. Investigate each stock before you buy.

4. Remember it is easier to buy than sell. The saleability of a stock is very important.

5. The market goes up slowly, but comes down fast.

6. Buy in a selling market - when nobody wants stock.

7. Sell in a buying market - when everybody wants stock.

8. The market is most dangerous when it looks best; it is most inviting when it looks worst.

9. Don't try to outguess the market.

10. Look out for buying fever; it is a dangerous disease.

11. Don't try to pick the bottom and top of the market.

12. Don't dream in the stock market; have some idea just how far your stock can go.

13. Remember the majority of traders are always buying at the top and selling at the bottom.

14. Don't worry over the profits you might have made.

15. Watch the news. Remember that the market actually is a barometer of business.

16. Don't buy fads or novelties - be sure the company you are becoming a partner in makes something everybody wants.

17. Don't treat loses lightly, they are serious. You are losing actual currency.

18. When you win don't get reckless; put your winnings in the bank for a while.

19. Don't talk about the market - you will attract too much idle gossip.

20. Fortunes are not made easily on Wall Street. Some professionals give their lives to the market and die poor.

21. Use your mistakes as object lessons - the person who makes the same mistake twice deserves no sympathy.

22. Money made easily in the market is never valued - easy come, easy go.

23. Don't blame the Stock Exchange for your mistakes.

24. Don't let emotion or prejudice warp your judgement. Base your operations on facts.

25. Avoid uncertainty. When the trend is in doubt, stay out.

26. Always favour the trade when fundamental and technical conditions co-operate.

THOUGHTS FROM T.T. HOYNE

1. Speculation is an art. The principle of every art is to have at the outset a clear conception of the end aimed at.

2. The second great general rule for successful speculation is, never enter upon any speculation without clearly conceiving precisely the amount of profit that is sought and exactly the amount of loss that will be submitted to in the effort to secure that profit.

3. Every speculator must think for himself.

4. A person must at all times strive to maintain the correct point of view towards the market in which he is trading. This contemplates the effect of the market on himself and other speculators; and their effect upon it.

5. A speculator should first determine never to do anything at all with a haste that precludes forethought.

6. A speculator must think for himself, and must do his thinking rigidly in accordance with the method of reasoning he laid down.

THOUGHTS AND RULES FROM VICTOR SPERANDEO.

1. Trade with a plan and stick to it.

2. Trade with the trend. "The trend is your friend"

3. Use stop losses wherever practical (mental ones if necessary)

4. When in doubt, get out!

5. Be patient. Never over-trade.

6. Let your profits run; cut your losses short.

7. Never let your profits run into a loss.

8. Buy weakness and sell strength. Be just as willing to sell as to buy.

9. Be an investor in the early stages of bull markets. Be a speculator in the latter stages of bull markets and in bear markets.

10.Never average a loss - don't add to a losing position.

11.Never buy just because the price is low. Never sell because the price is high.

12.Trade only in liquid markets.

13.Don't trade on the basis of tips. In other words "trade with the trend and not with your friend". Also, no matter how strongly you feel about a stock or other market, don't offer unsolicited tips or advice.

14.Always analyze your mistakes.

15.Your success depends on good execution.

16.Always keep your own records of your trades.

17.Know and follow the RULES!!

VICTOR SPERANDEO'S DEFINING CHARACTERISTICS OF BULL AND BEAR MARKETS

BULL MARKETS:
1. The median extent of primary bull markets is a 77.5% increase in prices from the previous bear market low point
.

2. The median duration of primary bull markets is 2 years and 4 months, or 2.33 years. 75% of all bull markets in history have lasted more than 657 days, (1.8 years) and 67% have lasted between 1.8 and 4.1 years.

3. The beginnings of bull markets are virtually indistinguishable from the last secondary reaction in the bear market until the passage of some time.

4. Secondary reactions in bull markets are *usually* marked by sharp rates of price decline relative to the preceding and ensuing price increases. In addition, the beginning of the reaction is usually marked by high volume, with lows made on low volume.

5. The confirmation date of a bull market is the date when prices in both the averages break above the high point of the last bear market correction and continue to move upward.

BEAR MARKETS:

1. The median extent of primary bull markets is a 29.4% decline from the previous bull market high, with 75% of all bear markets declining between 20.4% and 47.1%.

2. The median duration of bear markets is 1.1 years, with 75% of all bear markets lasting between 0.8 and 2.8 years.

3. The beginnings of bear markets *usually* follow a "test" of the previous bull market high on low volume followed by sharp declines on high volume. A "test" is when price levels closely approach but never reach the previous high point jointly. The low volume during this "test" is a key indication that confidence is at a low ebb and can easily turn into an abandonment of hopes upon which stocks were purchased at inflated prices.

4. After an extended bear swing, secondary reactions are usually marked by sudden and rapid advances followed by decreasing activity and the formation of a "line", which leads to slower declines to new lows.

5. The confirmation date of a bear market is the date when prices on both the averages break below the low point of the last bull market correction and continue to move downward. It is not atypical for one average to lag the other in time.

6. Intermediate bear market rallies are usually inverted "V" patterns where the low is made on high volume and the high is made on low volume.

UPWARD TREND: - An upward trend is a series of successive rallies that penetrate previous high points, interrupted by sell-offs or declines which terminate above the low points of the preceding sell-off. In other words, an uptrend is a price movement consisting of a series of higher highs and higher lows.

DOWNWARD TREND: - A downward trend is a series of successive declines which penetrate previous low points, interrupted by rallies or increases which terminate below the high points of the preceding rally. In other words, a downward trend is a price movement consisting of a series of lower lows and higher lows.

THE RELATION OF VOLUME TO PRICE MOVEMENTS: A market which has been overbought becomes dull on rallies and develops activity on declines; conversely, when a market is oversold, the tendency is to become dull on declines and active on rallies. Bull markets terminate in a period of excessive activity and begin with comparatively light transactions.

RELATIVE STRENGTH: - is simply a ratio between a single stock against a stock group or an average index, or between a stock group and a larger group of average index.

VICTOR SPERANDEO: Never buy a stock because it is cheap; the chances are that it is cheap for a good reason. What you want is a stock that is going to perform, that is going to appreciate in value faster than the average stock. Relative strength is a measure of this kind of performance. All things being equal, if you are looking to buy a stock, you should buy the *strongest* performers, as indicated by the best measurement of relative strength available.

VICTOR SPERANDEO: "There is an excellent correlation between rate of change of earnings growth and the change in the stock price."

Or re-formulated by Gordon Holmes "the slope of a given price trend almost always precedes the correspondent or equivalent earnings trend slope in time. The amount of time displacement is about three months".

VICTOR SPERANDEO: "Before asking, "What profit can I realize?" first ask, "What potential loss can I suffer?"

VICTOR SPERANDEO: "The way to build wealth is to preserve capital, make consistent profits, and *wait patiently* for the right opportunity to make extraordinary gains"

VICTOR SPERANDEO: "Never give back more than 50% of your gain"

HOW TO LOSE MONEY IN THE MARKETS – VICTOR NIEDERHOFFER

1. Know that you are the greatest, that winning is a foregone conclusion. Let your opponent know, by your words and deeds, that your winning is assured.

2. Excoriate the referee and insult his motives. He'll be so intimidated that he will never again call the close ones against you. Write a letter to a newspaper decrying the excessive level of regulation imposed by the SEC, and best of all the IRS. These agencies are filled with disinterested public servants. As long as the debate is engaged, they are happy.

3. Cut your gains when you are ahead. Relax, you're the greatest. Never think about what could go wrong and it won't. Grab at small profits and refuse to take losses.

4. When behind, put everything you have into catching up. After you're caught up, coast for a while and give yourself some well-deserved

praise. Dwell on your past victories, recalling them to yourself in precise detail. Never look back on your defeats, trying to figure out what you did wrong; that activity is for suckers. There's no need to learn from traders who have poor results: losses are just bad luck. The chances of lightning striking twice are remote.

5. Enrage your opponents by downplaying their chances and mocking their ability. Let your opponents know, a la Babe Ruth, exactly how you plan to trounce them: point to where you're going to hit. Let the market know your intentions.

6. Don't dignify the finals with any undue training that you wouldn't put forth in any other game. Nonchalance carries the day in the pinch. Don't worry about announcements or FED activities. How difficult can it be to make a few dollars trading?

7. Call a time-out when you have momentum, to cause your opponent to worry about what you're going to do next. When a market goes your way, get out immediately and think about what to do next. Limit your stock gains to two baggers.

8. Invite the opposite sex to the game and let it be known that you're the greatest and that you're saving the winning shot as your special shared secret. When trading, bring your favourite significant other by to see you in action. Hey, if you're good, flaunt it!!

9. Be sure to indulge in intercourse before you play. It will relax you and make you that much steadier in the pinch. If this diversion is not available, a few drinks or a nice big meal will do almost as well. Take a break with a paramour in the middle of the trading day.

10. Adapt new and experimental techniques for your crucial matches. You'll catch your opponent off guard. When in doubt, apply systems without paper trading.

11. Arrange to officiate when you have spare time during a tournament, or better still, accept a position on the committee. Don't be afraid to attend to other business while involved in a trade. Take your hand-

held quote machine to meetings, and trade around your positions during breaks.

12. Adopt expensive habits like playing polo or racing yachts. Be sure to make enough money trading each day to cover one special purchase.

13. If the score goes against you, stick to your guns. You know best. If the results go against you, don't worry. Gains are bound to come back, especially when the market is wrong.

14. Celebrate the victory the evening before, when you won't be too tired to enjoy it. Don't be afraid to tally your profits in a trade. Make sure you don't get less than your due. Don't even show up for trading the next day. Leave an order with your broker to exit at the close.

15. Forget about the frictions, the small wastes of energy that grind you down. Great strokes fell great oaks. Let your opponent worry about grabbing all the edges. Don't worry about your fills. What's a tick or two going to matter, anyway?

16. Even if these particular rules of losing don't apply, there are a million and one others available. Whether the pursuit is poker, sports, gambling or speculation, losing is the easiest thing in the world.

THE REVENGE FACTOR

- There's something important to know about losing, above and beyond the lessons it teaches you about winning. *After a loss, victory becomes more likely.*

- More on this subject from Rene Lacoste "I have often remarked that an unexpected defeat is generally followed by a series of successes; the best means of willing to win is to be beaten from time to time. That allows for better measurement of the meaning which separates the two expressions "to lose" and "to win", and that renews the desire to win. One is so made that one accustoms oneself more easily to success than to defeat; a series of victories seems always rapidly naturally to blunt the will. On the contrary, a defeat causes the well-known reaction: the desire to regain what one has just lost.

- It will be found sometimes that the player who has consistently lost sometimes wins, first one match then another, because by dint of being beaten has created with himself a greater desire to conquer

VICTOR NIEDERHOFFER: "In sports and markets, the most dangerous time is when you are ahead. That is when you most likely to let up, drop your guard, and make a bad decision out of overconfidence"

VICTOR NIEDERHOFFER: "The urge to get even is one of the most costly habits a speculator can have. Unfortunately, it is almost one of the most common. It's especially prevalent after a disastrous move. That's why, when prices make a huge move against you and then manage to come back, they're ready to go much further. At least that's what I always say when I lose 10 percent or 20 percent of my chips in a few days, wait until I'm close to even, and then exit my position in relief - only to see a continued move that would have garnered me a huge profit unfold in the seconds after I'm out. Some speculators could make fortunes by quantifying this tendency."

VICTOR NIEDERHOFFER: "The markets will punish you for every poor investment decision you make. Like a very hard master, it does not tolerate mistakes."

VICTOR NIEDERHOFFER: "Risk taking is one blade of the speculative scissors close to our hearts, is positively correlated with how well we feel about ourselves."

VICTOR NIEDERHOFFER: "Successful athletes, business executives and gambles alike spend the majority of their time and energy trying to discover and cultivate an advantage. In many cases, the fine line between success and failure is distinguished by an almost immeasurably small edge."

VICTOR NIEDERHOFFER: "In the face of danger, people will generally do what is instinctual as opposed to what is logical."

IMPORTANCE OF SELECTIVE SPECULATION
-JESSE LIVERMORE

- There is a time for all things, but I don't know it. And that is precisely what beats so many men in Wall Street who are very far from being in the main sucker class. There is a plain fool, who does all the wrong things everywhere, but there is the Wall Street fool, who thinks that he must trade all the time. No man can always have adequate reasons for buying and selling stocks daily - or sufficient knowledge to make his play an intelligent play.

On Mistakes and Wisdom:
- If a man did not make mistakes he would own the world in a month. But if he didn't profit by his mistakes he wouldn't own a blessed thing.

- Of course if a man is both wise and lucky, he will not make the same mistake twice. But he will make any one of the ten thousand brothers or cousins of the original. The mistake family is so large that there is always one of them around when you want to see what you can do in the fool-play line.

- A man can excuse his mistakes only by capitalizing on them to subsequent profit.

On the Speculator and his Emotions:
- I sometimes think that speculation must be an unnatural sort of business, because I find that the average speculator has arrayed against him his own nature. The weaknesses that all men are prone to are fatal to success in speculation-usually those very weaknesses that make him likeable to his fellows or that he himself particularly

guards against in those other ventures of his where they are not nearly so dangerous as when he is trading in stocks or commodities.

- The speculators chief enemy are always boring from within. It is inseparable from human nature to hope and to fear. In speculation when the market goes against you, you hope that every day will be the last day. It is absolutely wrong to gamble in stocks the way the average man does.

JESSE LIVERMORE "It never is your thinking that makes big money, it's the sitting"

THE THEOREMS OF DOW THEORY:

Theorem 1: There are 3 movements of the averages, all of which may be in progress at one and the same time. The first, and most important, is the primary trend: the broad upward or downward movements known as bull or bear markets, which may be of several years duration. The second, and most deceptive movement, is the secondary reaction: an important decline in a primary bull market or a rally in a primary bear market. These reactions usually last from three weeks to as many months. The third, and usually unimportant, movement is the daily fluctuation

Theorem 2: The primary movement is the broad basic trend generally known as a bull or bear market extending over periods which have varied from less than a year to several years. The correct determination of the direction of this movement is the most important factor in successful speculation. *There is no known method of forecasting the extent or duration of a primary movement.*

Theorem 3: A primary bear market is the long downward movement interrupted by important rallies. It is caused by various economic ills and does not terminate until stock prices have thoroughly discounted the worst that is apt to occur. There are three principal phases of a bear market: the first represents the abandonment of hopes upon which stocks were purchased at inflated prices; the second reflects selling due to decreased business and earnings, and the third is caused by distress selling of sound securities, regardless of their value, by those who must find a cash market for at least a portion of their assets.

Theorem 4: A primary bull market is a broad upward movement, interrupted by secondary reactions, and averaging longer than 2 years. During this time, stock prices advance because of a demand created by both investment and speculative buying caused by improving business conditions and increased speculative activity. There are 3 phases of a bull period: the first is represented by reviving confidence in the future of business; the second is the response of stock prices to the known improvement in corporations earnings; and the third is the period when speculation is rampant and inflation of stock prices apparent - a period when stocks are advanced on hopes and expectations.

Theorem 5: Secondary reactions: For the purpose of this discussion, a secondary reaction is considered to be an important decline in a bull market or advance in a bear market, usually lasting from 3 weeks to as many months, during which intervals the price movement generally retraces from 33% to 66% of the primary price change since the termination of the last preceding reaction. These reactions are frequently erroneously assumed to represent a change of primary trend, because obviously the first stage of a bull market must always coincide with a movement which might have proved to have been merely a secondary reaction in a bear market, the contra being true after the peak has been attained in a bull market.

SOME MARKET RULES - WILLIAM ENG:

1. Investment success is a slow climb uphill, but investment failure coasts quickly downhill. Money made quickly in the market will be inevitably lost because seldom are those who have the wisdom to

fall back to sound investment practices and rules after they have made a killing in the market.

2.   Learn to be patient. When a winning stock is recognized, be patient and wait for others to catch on to the same idea. It may take some time. While you are waiting for it to happen, do not get frustrated and sell out the position.

3.   Learn to recognize a steep ramp and subsequent fall in a stock price, which occurs over short periods, a couple of days. Such movements never hold once the peak is reached and will inevitably drop as fast as they have risen. When you see such a movement, sell at the top. Don't be tempted to hold onto the stock. Conversely, a sharp drop in share price, e.g. 10% overnight, (without underlying fundamental reasons), will inevitable produce a bounce back, the day after. Learn to buy into the bounce.

4.   We must go against our natural inclinations and learn to sell at the top and buy at the bottom. When markets are charging into new highs, we find that we get caught up in the fever of the bullishness. Because of this, we are insensitive to the fact that the market is most likely at the end of an extended run-up. The same situation occurs when markets are making new lows. When the markets are plummeting to new lows day after day, we find ourselves in a very bearish frame of mind. Instead of looking for value, we look to bail out of the losers.

5.   Conventional wisdom says that you cut your losses, but let your profits run. This is definitely true for trading, but some exceptions can be made when investing. If the market is down, and you have a loss in hand, but believe there is long term potential in the stock, then it is worth keeping it. Remember, investors are defined as those who buy and hold a stock, - until it delivers a profit. When this happens is not time related. This is because the money that is invested, is money that can be afforded to be lost and therefore is not immediately needed. Therefore the ability to hang onto positions exists. This assumes that good judgement has been initially made to choose a sound growth stock.

6. Learn to sit on your hands. Ironically most trades are not needed and it would be better to sit and wait and watch the market, rather than take action.

7. Markets move up. They move down. They go sideways or nowhere. There are no other patterns. Given these markets patterns, you should know when to get into the market or to stay out. In other words, learn when to wait and watch, and NOT ACT!!

8. We can be prone to one of two faults. Some of us act too quickly, often without much thought or consideration. Conversely, some of us act only after all the facts are in and only after spending considerable time deliberating these facts. Neither approach is really very good for helping you become a successful trader.

9. If you want to come out ahead, do not keep repeating your mistakes. This is the only way you will succeed.

10. As an investor, know your strong and weak points. For the vast majority of traders, successful or not, the problem of overriding is a weak point. Few traders have enough discipline to measure risk and limit market exposure by deliberately under trading. The same applies to investing. Know when to stay in the market, and when to get out.

11. Stocks are not human. Don't get emotionally attached to them. You can sell them without feelings of guilt or remorse.

12. No stock has ever gone up by itself. They need sponsors to bolster their prices. However, they have come down without any support.

13. Whatever is hard to do in the markets, is generally the right thing. Whatever is easy is usually the wrong thing to do.

14. Define market action first - then take appropriate action. In other words, develop a clear plan first of where you think the market is

going, and then execute against it. If the plan is vague and ill-conceived, the chances of it failing will be high.

WILLIAM NEIL'S WINNING SYSTEM: C-A-N-S-L-I-M

C = Current quarterly earnings per share. They must be at least 18% to 20%.

A = Annual earnings per share. They should show meaningful growth for the last five years.

N = New. Buy companies with new products, new management, or significant new changes in their industry conditions. And most important, buy stocks as they initially make new highs in price. (Forget cheap stocks, they are usually cheap for a very good reason).

S = Supply and Demand. There should be a small or reasonable number of shares outstanding, not large capitalization, older companies. And look for volume increases when a stock begins to move up.

L = Leaders. Buy market leaders, avoid laggards.

I = Institutional sponsorship. Buy stocks with a least a few institutional sponsors with better than average recent performance records.

M = The general market. It will determine whether you win or lose, so learn to interpret the daily general market indexes (price and volume changes) and action of the individual market leaders to determine the overall markets current direction.

WILLIAM NEIL: "The whole secret to winning in the stock market is to lose the least amount possible when you're not right".

WILLIAM NEIL: "Letting your losses run is the most serious mistake made by almost all investors. You positively must accept that mistakes in either timing or selection of stocks are going to be made by even the most professional investors."

WILLIAM NEIL: "In the stock market you absolutely can't win unless you have a strong predetermined defence to protect yourself against large losses. This may surprise you, but if you invest in stocks, you are going to make a never ending number of mistakes in your selection and timing of purchases.

These poor decisions will lead to losses, some of which can become quite awful. No matter how smart you may think you are or how good you believe your information or analysis is, you simply are not going to be right all of the time. In fact, you will probably be right only half the time."

WILLIAM NEIL: "It is far better to sell early. If you are not early, you will be late; you'll never sell at the exact top, so stop kicking yourself when a stock goes higher after you sell. The objective to make and take worthwhile gains and not get excited, optimistic or greedy as a stock's price advance gets stronger"

WILLIAM NEIL: "Investors who can be right and sit tight are uncommon. It takes time for a stock to make a big gain. Be patient. Achieving giant profits in a stock usually takes 1 - 3 years. "

WILLIAM NEIL: "Investors are always hoping rather than being realistic. You just can't afford to have a love affair with any stock"

INVESTOR MAGAZINE -FOCUS INVESTING

1. **INVEST ONLY IN OUTSTANDING COMPANIES**:- It makes sense to select the best companies for a focused portfolio because they will usually have a history of stable management and superior operating and market performance that should be capable of being replicated

in the future. Growing, consistently profitable companies generally produce predictable earnings, the only type capable of being soundly valued. Let your investment strategy be driven by the operating results and progress of your companies, not by day to day movements in share prices.

2. **FIND ONLY 5 to 10 SENSIBLY PRICED COMPANIES**:- There aren't that many really outstanding companies. Why sink your money into those that are only second best? Phil Fisher, one of the great growth company investors of all time said: "I knew the more I understood about the company the better off I would be. Great stocks are extremely hard to find. I knew I wanted to win the best or none at all." Fisher has held big positions in growing, profitable companies like Motorola and Texas Instruments since the 1950's - and has made a fortune by doing so.

3. **PLACE BIG BETS ON HIGH PROBABILITY EVENTS**:- Over-diversification in a stock portfolio is a hedge against ignorance. When you come across a very attractive opportunity, the only reasonable course of action is to make a large investment. Why invest at all in a marginal or unattractive prospect? No reason - but many investors do. Charlie Munger, Buffett's partner sums it up nicely: "I would say that if our predictions have been a little better than other peoples it's because we've tried to make fewer of them. The wise ones bet heavily when the world offers them a great opportunity. They bet big when they have the odds. And, the rest of the time, they don't. It's just that simple.

4. **BE PATIENT**:- Among all active strategies, Focus investing stands the best chance of outperforming index returns over time but investors need to be patient and hold on to their carefully selected investments even when it seems that other strategies are delivering better market performance. In the short term, investor's emotions - fear and greed - dominate stock market activity. As the time horizon lengthens, the trend in the economies of the underlying business will increasingly determine the share price.

5. **DON'T PANIC OVER PRICE CHANGES**:- Market price fluctuations are an inevitable part of Focus investing. Diversification may have the effect of averaging out the inevitable short term shifts in the prices of individual stocks, but, long term performance will suffer. Focus investors put up with the short term bumps in market prices because the know that in the long run, the underlying economics of the companies they have chosen will more than compensate for these short term fluctuations.

Chapter 2: A Basic Guide to Day Trading

Quote Services:
Good real time, streaming, tick-by-tick quotes are essential for day trading. We don't recommend attempting to day trade without the proper tools.

Brokers:
A good broker is a must for day trading. You need to have fast, timely executions. Nothing is worse than not knowing if you are in or out of a position. We cannot emphasize this enough. Bad executions can cost you a lot of money. Check out a broker before you use them or get recommendations from people that have used for day trading. Investin.co.uk caters to day-traders and offers a quote/execution package at a reasonable rate. They also answer their phones. A big plus when you are in a jam. While investigating a potential broker, try calling the broker several times during busy market hours. See if they answer on the first ring, or if you are put on hold 10 minutes. This is important because if you cannot execute your order via the Internet for unforeseen reasons, you can execute it via a phone call. Other things you want to look for are: Fast Executions for stocks, Fast Confirmation, Price, Check Writing Privileges etc.

Stop Losses:
Always follow stop losses when day trading. We have seen many day traders ride a £500 loss to a £5000 loss. A good trader calmly takes a small loss and goes onto the next trade. Remember that trading capital is our business; if it burns to the ground we don't have insurance. We use a -10 - 20p stop loss on all trades. Some traders have tolerance for pain and use larger stop losses - that is perfectly fine. The most important thing is to know where you will get out before you get in. Have a plan and stick with it. Day trading is not an exact science but you must have reasonable rules and ALWAYS follow them. Once we are in a trade, the next challenge becomes when to sell. Below are the strategies that we use to try to optimize profits and limit losses. Every trader must determine their own risk level that is comfortable. You may do this on your

own or by discussing it with your broker. Below we describe many commonly used exit strategies:

Exiting a Losing Trade:

We use 10 - 20p as a stop loss for all trades. This means if a stock trades down below -10 - 20p where we bought it we would sell. You may use "programmed" stops if they are offered by your broker. (Some brokers do not offer this.) If given the option, we would rather choose to watch the trade in REAL TIME and try to exit trades manually. In other words...simply by watching the tape, and entering the order when in our stop loss range. The reason for this is that you do not want a market maker taking a stock down just to hit your stop...it's like showing your hand at a poker game. Both ways are acceptable...and both work. Just be aware of the differences.

Exiting a Profitable trade:

There are two ways we exit our winning trades to maximize our profits. These are only two of many trade management techniques. Take your profits as you see fit. Remember it is YOUR TRADE, you must manage it. No one else can do it for you.

Trailing Stop Loss:

We place a trailing stop loss at -10 to 20p below the current price. As price of the stock moves up, the stop follows your position up throughout the day to lock in your profits. This strategy helps you to maximize profits by letting winners run. Most on-line brokers DO NOT allow you to enter a "programmed" trailing stop loss into their system. To use this strategy you MUST watch the stock yourself throughout the day adjust your trailing stop "mentally" as the stock moves up. Or you must continuously place "stop" orders with your broker...cancel, change them, move them and re-enter as the stock moves up. Once again, we treat day trading as a business...and encourage watching all your trades in real time. Another commonly used method is to sell 1/2 your position when you are comfortable with the profits...and let the rest continue to "trade"...and then placing an appropriate stop (determined by you) on the balance of the position.

End of Day:
If not stopped out by a stop loss, or a trailing stop loss, we will ALWAYS EXIT all trades before the market closes.

Holding Positions Overnight:
Some traders are comfortable holding positions overnight. We DO NOT recommend for day trading. The reason is because day traders tend to hold concentrated (a large number of shares) of one stock. Once the market closes, we lose control over that stock. We are now at the mercy of overnight news, conditions etc... Our long position could easily open 9 points lower on unexpected news. Leave the long term positions to the Fund Managers and long term investors.

Buy Points:
We always adhere to a precise buy point. What this means is we DO NOT buy the stock until it has traded at or through a BUY. We use the buy point as a confirmation, a signal. If it doesn't reach the buy, we don't jump the gun. There will be plenty of profitable trades. Also, once a stock begins to approach its buy, we will watch very carefully how it trades. Is the bid size larger than the ask size? How is it trading? Do we see a lot of buyers at the ask? Do we see sellers? All of this will help determine if a trade looks like it will be a good one. Now, no one has a crystal ball...but paying attention to how a stock is trading will certainly help you make more profitable buys.

How to "read" the tape:
By watching "time and sales" we can learn a lot about how a stock trades. As we watch each trade go by on our quote service you can see whether demand is picking up or slowing down. This is a form of tape reading and it takes some time to learn, but is crucial to being a good day trader. Are there more trades at the bid or the ask...in other words are there more buyers or sellers. Also, look at the volume of the trades by size...are they 1000 shares, 100 shares, large blocks? This can also help you if there are enough serious buyers interested to move the stock. Also, you want to watch for a stock gaining momentum...meaning is it starting to trade more rapidly? Or does it just seem drifty? Momentum moves stocks...so if there are enough buyers (or sellers) a stock

may languish. Or does a stock have a lot of attention, but does not up-tick? This could be an indication of weakness, or that there is lot of stock for sale at the ask. Also, keep track of the Bid Size and Ask Size. If the Size is larger than the Ask Size this may indicate (not always) that the stock is. For example if the Bid Size is 5000 and the Ask Size is 1000, this may indicate more strength than if the Bid Size is 1000 and Ask Size is 5000. Remember this is not "absolute" but merely an indicator to take into account. If all this seems confusing to you, try this simple exercise. Pull up a quote of any stock...try to make it a stock that has a good daily range...like Vodafone or BT and every 5 minutes monitor the bid, ask for the bid size and ask for the size of a stock. Track it throughout the day. It is a bit tedious but it will help you to learn how to "read" the tape. You will know how a stock acts when it is "strong" and how a stock acts when it is "weak".

Trade Size:
The size of your day-trading account, the risk level you are comfortable with, the number of opportunities at hand on any given day, etc....Only you can determine these. Day-traders will trade 1000, 500, 300, or even 200 shares of any one stock at a time. A rule of thumb is not to use more than 3% of your capital on any one trade. For example: If your portfolio is £20,000...do not risk more £600 on any one trade. More simply put, one stock at a time. A rule of thumb that is sometimes used is do not risk do not lose more than £600 on one. Try not to put all of your eggs in one basket. For example, if presented with 3-4 trading opportunities we will try to spread out our capital to try to take advantage of as much as we can. This optimizes our profit potential.

Homework:
Remember to always do your homework. We suggest you check any and all news, consult your broker before making any investment decisions. Remember, this is money and you are responsible for it.

Shorting:
When you short a stock you sell a stock first and then buy it back later. How do you do this? Your brokerage house allows you to borrow the shares, which allows you to sell them first. You must buy them back or

"cover" in order to close out the trade. In other words you are betting that the price of the stock is going to go down. There are MANY RULES involved in shorting. These involve uptick rules, shares available to short, margin requirements, holding shorts overnight etc....Only your broker can answer these questions about their policies and procedures. As with all or trading, DO NOT short until you understand all the risks and rules and get advice from a licensed professional.

Chasing:
If you miss a buy point because a stock is moving too fast or because of broker problems, is it OK .to pay more for it? The answer is yes and no. We do not recommend chasing stocks up. The reason behind this is because we want to position ourselves at a good, safe level. If we can't buy in at that level, the trade becomes riskier. Having said that, everyone has a different tolerance for pain. If you think a stock is really running, paying a small amount more than the buy point may work out. This is completely your decision, and is considered risky. NEVER chase a stock 1/2 to 1 point above your buy point. If you miss it that much, let it go. There will always be other trades. DON'T CHASE.

Equity Investment Strategies

Chapter 3: Tips for Traders

JACK SCHWAGERS ADVICE for TRADING OPTIONS, FUTURE AND DERIVATIVES

1. Be sure you really want to trade. Know yourself well

2. Examine your motives and think about why you want to trade. Don't trade for the wrong reasons.

3. Match your trading method to your personality. Make sure your find your right comfort level

4. It is absolutely necessary to have an edge. If you don't know what your edge is, you haven't got one.

5. To have an edge you must have a method. With the method goes an edge.

6. Developing a method is hard work. There are no short-cuts to trading success. You may hit many dead ends before you come up with a successful formula

7. Skill versus hard work. Competent trading can be learnt through hard work, but to be a superior trader you must have raw talent. Some do and some don't. Be realistic in your goals

8. Good trading should be effortless. If the preparation is outstanding the implementation will be effortless

9. Money management is critical to control the amount of risk. In other words, protect your capital in order to come back and fight another day

10. You must have a trading plan: a combination of trading method, specific money management and trade entry

11.Discipline: You must have it and show it. Without it you are lost

12.Understand that you are responsible for your actions. Win or lose, you have to bear the brunt of your own decisions

13.You need to be independent and do your own thinking. Don't follow the herd and get caught up in mass hysteria

14.Confidence: an unwavering belief in yourself and your own abilities is an almost universal characteristic amongst master traders.

15.Losing is part of the game.

16.Trade only when you feel confident and optimistic. You don't HAVE to trade. You can take a time-out and sit on the sidelines and watch the market.

17.The urge to seek advice. If you find yourself with the urge to seek someone else's advice, stop trading. It betrays a lack of self-confidence.

18.The virtue of patience. Waiting for the right moment to buy and sell increases the probability of success.

19.The importance of sitting. Patience is critical in staying the distance with trades that work. Don't be shaken out early.

20.Develop a low risk idea.

21.The importance of varying bet size. Vary your bet size according to how well you are trading. If confidence is down, you can trade with 100X lower amounts, rather than getting out of the market completely.

22.Scaling in and out of trades. You down have to get in and out of a position all at once.

23.Being right is more important than being a genius. Think about winning rather than trying to be a hero. You can't pick the exact point of bottoms and tops of markets, so don't try to be perfect, rather aim for a time- after-time consistent trading record.

24.Don't worry about looking stupid.

25.Sometimes action is more important than prudence.

26.Catching part of the move is just fine. See 23.

27.Maximize gains and not the number of wins.

28.Learn to be disloyal. Don't fall in love with a stock
.

29.Pull out partial profits. Pull a portion of winnings out of the market, to prevent trading discipline from deteriorating into complacency.

30.Hope is a four letter word.

31.Don't do the comfortable thing. Human tendency is to select the comfortable route. Learn to recognize the signs and not fall into the trap.

32.You can't win if you have to win. If you risk losing money you can't afford to lose, then all the pitfalls of trading will be magnified.

33.Think twice when the market lets you off the hook easily. Check your position to see if there is a change of direction that you might be able to benefit from.

34.A mind is a terrible thing to close. Those who excel at trading have an open-mind. They are flexible in their thinking and are prepared to change positions quickly.

35.The markets are expense places to look for excitement. Excitement has a lot to do with the image of trading but nothing to do with success in trading, except in an inverse sense.

36.The calm state of a trader. There is an emotional state associated with the successful trade that is the antithesis of excitement.

37.Identify and eliminate stress. Stress in trading is a sign that something is wrong.

38.Pay attention to intuition. Intuition is simply experience that resides in the subconscious mind. Listen to it when it talks to you!!

39.Life's mission and love of the endeavour. Does trading fill this role for you?

40.Prices are non-random - the market can be beaten.

41.There is more to life than trading.

Chapter 4: Some Memorable Quotes and Thoughts

OLD WALL STREET ADAGE "Scared money never wins"

DRUCKENMILLER: "When you have tremendous conviction in a trade, you have to go for the jugular. It takes courage to be a pig."

NATHAN ROTHCHILD'S RULE FOR SUCCESS: "I never buy at the bottom and I always sell too soon."

AN OLD SAYING: "Bulls make money and bears make money, but pigs don't."

JOE KENNEDY (father of JFK): "Only a fool holds out for the top dollar."

A GREAT TRADER once said "There are only 2 emotions in the market, hope and fear. The only problem is we hope when we should fear, and fear when we should hope"

BERNARD BERUCH, the financier "Repeatedly I have sold a stock while it was rising, - and that has been one reason why I have held on to my fortune. Many a time, I might have made a good deal more by holding a stock, but I would also have been caught in the fall, when the price of the stock collapsed"

OLD JAPANESE PROVERB "Making money is like digging with a needle in the sand; losing money is like pouring water on the sand"

LAO-TSU: "He who knows much about others may be learned, but he who understands himself is more intelligent. He who controls others may be more powerful, but he who has mastered himself is mightier still."

BERNARD BERUCH, the financier "If a speculator is correct half of the time he is hitting a good average. Even being right 3 or 4 times out of

10, should bring a person a fortune if he has the sense to cut his losses quickly on the ventures where he has been wrong."

ROCKNE "These are the weaknesses which you must systematically work on until you can change and build them up into your strong points"

WILLIAM O'NEIL "Remember the objective is not to be right, but to make big money when you are right"

EMMANUEL LASKER, World Chess Champion: "When you see a good move, wait - look for a better one" One can always be more informed, more prepared and better equipped to make a decision.

PAUL TUDOR JONES "Don't be a hero. Don't have an ego. Always question yourself and your ability. Don't ever feel you are very good. The second you do, you are dead."

GARFIELD DREW: "Stocks do not sell for what they are worth, but for what people think they are worth"

JAMES L FRASER: "There are no certainties in this investment world, and where there are no certainties, you should begin by understanding yourself"

FRANK J.WILLIAMS: "If you are intelligent the market will teach you caution and fortitude, sharpen your wits and reduce your pride. If you are foolish and refuse to learn a lesson, it will ridicule you, laugh you to scorn, break you, and toss you on the rubbish-heap"

THOMAS TEMPLETON HOYNE "The law of an organized, or psychological crowd is mental unity. The individuals composing the crowd lose their conscious personality under the influence of emotion and are ready to act as one, directed by the low, crowd intelligence."

JOHN SCHULTZ "The guiding light of investment contrarianism is not that the majority view - the conventional, or received, wisdom, is always wrong. Rather, it's that majority opinion tends to solidify into a dogma while its basic premises begin to lose their original validity and so become progressively more mispriced in the marketplace"

J.R.CAPABLANCA, World Chess Champion, 1921. "There have been many times in my life when I came near to thinking that I could not lose a single game. Then I would be beaten and the lost game would bring me back from dreamland to earth. Nothing is as healthy as a thrashing at the proper time, and from few won games have I learned so much as I have from most of my defeats."

GALTON on herd behaviour "An incapability of relying on oneself and faith in others are precisely the conditions that compel brutes to live in herds. The vast majority of people have a natural tendency to shrink from the responsibility of standing and acting alone. They exalt the *vox populi* even when they know it to be the utterance of a mob of nobodies"

WISWELL, a checkers master, wrote these thoughts that equally apply to investment strategies:

"Only those with passion become masters"

"Success does not come all at once; even for masters it comes in stages, separated by years.

"You are the architect of your own victories and defeats."

"Some players not only go down to defeat, they run halfway to meet it"

"In order to win, you should analyze the play, you need to analyze the player, and you must, above all, analyze yourself."

"When all is said, superior knowledge is the mightiest weapon of the masters. One does blunder, perhaps must blunder, now and then; but prepared analysis, classical or contemporary, is nonetheless one's chief asset in the larger struggle for the world titles."

"The master knows the right time to do nothing"

"If you have foresight, you will probably win; if you have insight, you will probably draw; if you have hindsight, you will probably lose. And we all win, draw and lose."

"There are players who keep an "open mind" and are ready, when necessary, to change course and improvise, in order to win or draw, then there are others who have a rigid mindset, and plough ahead, regardless of the consequences. The latter philosophy, or lack of philosophy, often leads to defeat."